D1590711

# LAMB TO THE SLAUGHTER

# LAMB TO
# THE SLAUGHTER

*by*

## BROTHER GEORGE EVERY
### S.S.M.

JAMES CLARKE & CO. LTD.
33 Store Street
LONDON, W.C.1

First published 1957

MADE AND PRINTED IN GREAT BRITAIN BY
THE GARDEN CITY PRESS LIMITED
LETCHWORTH, HERTFORDSHIRE

FOR
NORMAN AND YVONNE
NICHOLSON

July 5th, 1956

# Contents

# Contents

# Introduction

THIS book finds its occasion in an invitation to deliver passiontide lectures at the Bishop's Hostel, Lincoln. These are given to the students year by year before they share with the rest of the congregation of Lincoln Minster in the commemoration of the passion and resurrection of Christ. They are neither devotional addresses nor lectures on the doctrine of the atonement in a theological course. But they are addressed to theological students, and intended to provide material for reflection on the mystery of the passion.

When I was asked to give these lectures in 1955, I brought to their preparation a particular concern which had been on my mind for a long time. It first began when I was a schoolboy and browsed in *The Golden Bough*. Then, or soon after, I discovered Jane Harrison's *Ancient Art and Ritual*, and her *Prolegomena to the*

*Study of Greek Religion.* These books were intended by their authors to demonstrate a close connection between all religion and magical rites intended to make the corn grow tall, lettuces large, babies bonny, calves and lambs sturdy. They did not attempt to establish a direct affiliation between Christianity and the mystery religions, where such ritual was given a spiritual sense, and rites intended to promote birth and physical growth were sublimated to encourage rebirth and spiritual growth in another form or in another world. But the parallels were at least indicated, and I knew how many people believed that the Catholic faith was the medieval form of agricultural magic, soon to be superseded by exact science.

The effect on myself was otherwise. I found the study of ritual imaginatively engaging. The interpretation of magic as primitive science seemed to me to be based on a misunderstanding of religion. Supplications to the Great Mother and her children were represented as naïve, clumsy attempts to produce assured results. I had, and still have, some sympathy with those who deplore the decay of natural religion in Christendom, the slow disappearance of ancient pieties towards holy things and places under the influence, first of the Church, then of the Reformation, and then of science. This regret is common to many poets, and has found radical expression in our time in the passion of W. B. Yeats for the Celtic twilight, of D. H. Lawrence for the dark gods, and of Robert Graves for his White Goddess. It appears in a modified form in some Christians, notably in the writings of Professor C. S. Lewis. But while I still regret the misrepresentation of pagan religion by some modern rationalists, and some ancient and modern Christians, I have come to understand that modern science is an inevitable consequence of the Jewish and Christian division between God and creation. If we go back behind that, and see divinity in the creatures, we shall find ourselves in a world of demons, demons in stars, demons in atoms. To Professor Lewis the gulf between Christian and pagan is slight in comparison with the chasm between Christian and post-Christian man.[1] But this view seems to reduce the reality and the permanence of the change that was wrought in man by the incarnation of Christ. Modern man is more truly a child of Christendom than medieval man, whose imagination was still partly pagan. Professor Lewis writes in a spirit of fun: "It would be pleasant to see some future Prime Minister—say Mr. Attlee—trying to kill a large and lively milk-white bull in Westminster Hall. But we shan't." I wish that I were quite so sure of this. I believe that our best defence against the return of irrational and idolatrous religions lies in the continued health of the spirit of iconoclasm which the philosopher and the scientist have inherited from the theologians, not only from Protestant theologians, but from medieval scholastics and mystics who taught and practised care and reserve in all that we think or say about God. At least we can be sure that an idolatrous religion established by a

[1] See his inaugural lecture at Cambridge on November 29th, 1954, published under the title, *De Descriptione Temporum*, 1955.

totalitarian regime will be resisted by sceptics and Christians in common.

Among reflective agnostics who have pondered on the problem of Christian origins the Christian faith may be regarded as a survival of primitive religion, or as a stage in the development of the scientific attitude to nature and the world. These views shade into one another. The theologian must speak to both of them. His temptation is to evade the problem of the relation of Christianity to other kinds of religion. This is not only a problem of historical origins, but of the place of the mythological imagination in Christian thinking.

Sir James Frazer and Miss Harrison were largely, though not exclusively, concerned with agricultural religion. They were right in perceiving certain uniformities in the attitude of the farmer to beasts and plants, and to the cycle of the seasons, from the first foundation of the Babylonian cities to the agricultural and industrial revolutions. But they failed to observe how much in his religious practice was taken over directly from earlier hunters and fishermen. Animal sacrifice is a case in point. Frazer tended to regard the beast as a substitute for a king or a headman. Miss Harrison was more aware that he had a sanctity of his own, inherited from a time when bulls were more masterful than men. This has become clearer as we have discovered more of the art and religion of palaeolithic man. We know now that the idea of a sacred victim whose blood renews the earth and the air and the vitality of men and beasts is rather the cause than the consequence of agricultural practice, and that sacrifice is older than a particular way of life.

That sacrifice is older than any other religious institution is implied in the Biblical tradition that is common to Israel and Christendom. In the Bible particular instructions are given for particular sacrifices, but the institution itself is taken for granted. The sacrificial idea persists from Abel to Noah, from Noah to the Patriarchs, and reappears in the varying forms of the Mosaic ordinances. As we shall see in the body of these lectures, there are significant differences between Jewish and other sacrifices, but the Christian doctrine of the sacrifice of Christ is coloured not only by recollections of the Old Testament, but by the general notion of sacrifice as it was understood in the ancient world, and more especially in the immediate environment of the infant Church.

The further development of the sacrificial idea in Christendom has led to conflict and tension, partly because different nations had already a different understanding of the idea itself before their first conversion, but even more because liturgical practice determines the development of doctrine. The structure of the mass in the Middle Ages, for instance, determined not only the doctrine of the eucharist, but also in a great degree the dominant ideas of sacrifice and atonement in Western theology. Yet much in that structure was shaped by practical circumstances, as rites originally intended for central Italy in the fourth and fifth centuries were adapted to the different circumstances of the British Isles and the north of Europe, where Latin was not understood, and brought back in their new forms to the south as the differences slowly developed between liturgical Latin and the different forms of Romance speech. Because the mass had become, in the eyes of Western Europeans, a rite performed by a priest, with some help from servers, for hearers who might better be described as spectators, the sacrifice of Christ on the cross and in the mass was conceived as a work wrought for us. As the priest offered, so Christ suffered, not only on our behalf but in our place. The doctrine of substitution in this sense grows naturally out of Low mass, without any general communion, recited and performed before a congregation, and generally with some special intention.

Substitution in another sense is involved in the idea of sacrifice. The victim and the offerer are identified. The saving victim is the divine image. So Christ on the cross is God and Man, not only an oblation for the sins of the whole world, but the supreme revelation of the love of God. His wounds and His words tell us the secrets that despairing men and women sought in the torn entrails of sacrificed birds and beasts. At the same time they call us to share in His sacrifice, carry His cross, to suffer, die, and rise again with Him and in Him.

The Christian revelation is given in the language of sacrifice. To that extent Frazer and Miss Harrison were perfectly right. They implied, though they did not state, that Christianity is a development of agricultural magic. Modern anthropologists would prefer to say that agricultural religion and magic develop out of the pre-magical rituals of the hunt. As agricultural religion includes pre-agricultural elements, so Christianity, considered as a religion, includes elements derived from agricultural and hunting rites. But all these are not borrowings. Those who wish to remove the language of sacrifice from their interpretation of the life and death of Christ would "demythologize" the story of His passion by removing not only the resurrection, but the institution of the eucharist. What is left may still have a point, and may still be associated with some interpretations of some parts of

S. Paul's epistles, but it can hardly be regarded as the same gospel to which the early Christians committed themselves. The evidence for their belief in the importance of Christ's resurrection is too strong.

Objections to belief in the resurrection on grounds of historical evidence, must fairly and squarely be faced. But on this question, the possibility of any decision will depend on our opinion of the relevance of this decision, of the sense and significance of the question. The contention of these lectures is that our understanding of the issues involved in Christian belief depends, at least in part, on our general estimate of the idea of sacrifice. Is it a psychological disease, a discarded stage in the development of agricultural science, or something rooted in the nature of things?

# Chapter I: The Origins of Sacrifice

SACRIFICE is for us a very difficult idea. The Bible takes it for granted as part of any normal human life, as much as eating, drinking, and sleeping, birth, marriage, and death. The Greek and Latin classical writers, with a few eccentric exceptions, do the same. The starting point of Indian and Chinese philosophy is to be found in commentaries upon sacrificial rites[1] which were already old, mysterious, puzzling, in need of enlightened exegesis. Confucius declared that "whoso understood the meaning of the Great Sacrifice could grasp the cosmic system as clearly as if it were lying on the palm of his hand."[2] But in our own religion there is only one sacrifice,

[1] See C. Dawson, *Religion and Culture*, 1948, pp. 92–5.
[2] Quoted in R. Wilhelm, *A Short History of Chinese Civilization*, Eng. trans., 1929, p. 109.

the cross of Christ, remembered, recalled, represented, even in some sense, as some say, repeated in the sacrament of the eucharist. The idea of sacrifice has been narrowed to a particular aspect of the redemption and of the Holy Communion, and in theological discussion of this aspect the meaning of the word has become exceedingly fluid. When we say that the eucharist is "a true and proper sacrifice" and the cross "propitiatory" we use these words in a meaning peculiar to a particular eucharistic theology and a particular theology of the atonement. We may indeed believe that our meaning is based on the Bible, but we come to the Bible with our own theological ideas already framed, whereas the Bible takes sacrifice for granted as a universal human institution, older than Noah and Abraham, older even than the first murder.[1]

The popular use of the word seems at first sight to make confusion worse confounded. We speak of "sales at a sacrifice," when goods are offered on the counter to placate the anger and gain the

[1] Genesis 4, vv. 3–4.

20

favour of the customer. We speak also of self-sacrifice as a quality in lives, devoted to young children, to old parents, to a mission or a cause. Death in battle is the "supreme sacrifice"; sometimes sacrifices are said to be "senseless." The common idea is one of waste, but not of final waste, of a loss, in goods or life, that may or will become profit for someone at some future time. Sacrifice in this secular sense is seldom given to a god, but it is "made sacred" in that someone or something is set on one side, made taboo or untouchable, consecrated to an end or purpose that is not immediate or obvious, and may prove on closer scrutiny unreal or imaginary.

The roots of this notion lie deep. We seek for its sources in the shadowy past, beyond and behind the historical religions, in an age when men and animals lived a common life. Edwin Muir writes of this in his sensitive autobiography:

That age is fabulous to us, populated by heraldic men and legendary beasts. We see a reflection of it in the Indian reliefs where saints and crowned emperors wander among tigers, elephants, and

monkeys, and in the winged bulls of the Assyrians
with their human heads: angel, beast, and man in
one. The age which felt this connection between
men and animals was so much longer than the brief
historical period known to us that we cannot con-
ceive it; but our unconscious life goes back into it.
In that age . . . the creatures went about like
characters in a parable of beasts. Some of them
were sacred and some monstrous, some quaint and
ugly as house gods; they were worshipped and
sacrificed; they were hunted, and the hunt, like the
worship and the sacrifice, was a ritual act. . . .
As their life had to be taken and the guilt for it
accepted, the way of taking it was important, and the
ritual arose, in which were united the ideas of necessity and guilt, turning the killing into a mystery.[1]

In order to understand the notion of
sacrifice we have to go back before history,
before literature, before agriculture, to
find the roots of relationships between
men and beasts which precede what we
now call the domestication of animals.
The very phrase itself suggests stables,
kennels, and hutches, but anyone who has
seen a Greek or an Arab shepherd going
after goats in mountainous country, or a
swineherd in scrub in Serbia, will know

[1] *An Autobiography*, 1954, pp. 47–8; also in *The Story
and the Fable*, 1940.

that man does not always take the lead, and must have been in times past the followers, not the leader, as Lapps still follow their reindeer.

Many theologians distrust anthropology for valid reasons. The material is so vast that it provides ample opportunities to discover and collect facts that will support a particular hypothesis. The early history of the science of comparative religion, like the history of modern psychology, is a tale of warring sects. But in the last twenty years this science has been moving on to more secure ground. Anthropologists are no longer so dependent on the evidence of Australian aborigines who do not understand their questions, and Red Indians who have a shrewd idea of what kind of answer will best please the inquirer. The primary material for the study of primitive religion has been enlarged by the exploration of palaeolithic art, and especially of painting and sculpture in the great caves of southern France and the north of Spain. Altamira, it is true, was first discovered as long ago as 1879, but its significance was not realized until other caves were explored in the first years of this century. The new discoveries at Lascaux in and after 1940, and the patient labours of the Abbé Breuil, have put us on the track of clues which enable a great deal of scattered material to be placed for the first time in an intelligible context.

This material comes from the last Ice Age, when, as the geologists explain to us, a thick sheet of ground ice covered the British Isles and the North Sea, Scandinavia, and a great part of Germany. Arctic or semi-Arctic flora and fauna abounded in France, Spain, and Italy. It is generally agreed that this age ended about 10000 B.C. The time of its beginning is a more difficult question. Some authorities would put the first Aurignacian remains at 80000; others would not go beyond 20000 B.C. The Abbé Breuil speaks of "four hundred centuries." Even if we halve or quarter this figure, we are left with an age longer than the whole history of agriculture.[1]

[1] See a table in J. Bandi and H.-J. Maringer, *Art in the Ice Age*, London, 1953, p. 8.

We now have enough caves to make some cautious generalizations. It is as if we had rediscovered a handful of classical temples or Gothic cathedrals of various periods, with a minimum of liturgical implements, but with much of the wall decoration more or less intact. We can now make some sense of a large number of small objects found at different times in sites of the same period, incised weapons and tools, statuettes and amulets, and occasional sketched and painted stones. Most of the drawings and paintings found in the large caves are of great beasts, bear, elk, bison, horses, rhinoceros, reindeer, elephants, either in the act of reproduction, or at the point of death, with arrows and spears in their sides. They are so placed that they cannot be seen without great difficulty, at the end of long winding passages, far away from any natural light. They are often drawn and painted on top of one another. They can hardly be interpreted as art in any ordinary sense, though they are often executed with extraordinary skill and verve. They cannot have been made for the pleasure or instruction of human spectators. They must be addressed either to the beasts themselves or to their guardian spirits.

It now seems to be agreed that they are part of a ritual connected in the minds of those who made them with the preservation and slaughter of great game. The hunter then and now loves his game. If he kills indiscriminately, the supply will disappear. It is as important to him that the beasts should increase and multiply in the breeding season, as that they should die when he needs to renew his strength by devouring flesh. The evidence of palaeolithic painting powerfully suggests that the hunter felt a reverence and wonder before the beasts as in some important respects superior in strength, agility, and skill to his humdrum self. He slew them to share their strength. In one particular only was he their superior. He could understand them as they could not understand him. He knew their style of action through and through.

When he painted their great forms charging, pierced with arrows, falling in the agony of death, was he trying to persuade them to surrender, to fall into his snare, which he sometimes drew over them in the shape which archaeologists call a "tectiform"? In other words, was he making magic, luring them on to will their own death? This explanation has some support. Men are sometimes represented in the paintings and drawings clad in the skins of beasts, seeking by skill and cunning perhaps to imitate and learn their movements, perhaps to deceive their quarry by disguising their own scent. But some of these figures on closer examination will be found to represent not a man but a monster, a spirit of the wild. In one he seems to be playing a pipe. His music gathers beasts and men for birth, copulation, and death. Moreover, in one of the caves, at Laussel, a small image of a great lady is carved in low relief, heavy with young, bearing a bison's horn. She is of the earliest period of cave art, the Aurignacian, and resembles numerous tiny statuettes of maternal figures, brooding over children, which have been found in sites of the same period all over Europe and Western Asia.

The beasts were drawn and painted not in the open air, where it might conceivably be expected that magic rites would affect their minds, but in the heart of the earth. The artists, if we may use such a word, would seem to be addressing not a human audience, or an animal audience, but the rock, the earth from which they were hewn, the mother of plants and beasts and seasons, of all living.

If the experts are right, these paintings are part of a ritual action, which in one instance at least involved a mimetic representation of the actual hunt. At Montespan in the Haute-Garonne a clay model of a headless bear has been found,[1] with an actual bear's head lying between his paws, probably the last of a whole series of bears' heads struck off the model in what may be called a ritual rehearsal. Elsewhere human figures appear in a stooping posture, as if to execute some ritual action in the cave. Sometimes at least they are masked. At this point we may use, with considerable caution, the evidence of ritual dances by Australian

[1] Bandi and Maringer, *op. cit.*, p. 90.

aborigines, often fantastically robed and masked, in connection with the retouching of certain paintings on rock surfaces. These are crude and hieratic by comparison with the palaeolithic examples. They are said to represent certain desirable fruits, and the powers that supply rainfall. These *wondjinas* must be kept in good condition, or the rain will not fall. They are human faces, with eyes and noses, but no mouths, for if they had mouths it would rain all the time.[1] This is pure magic, a particular formula to produce a particular effect. It does not follow that the cave paintings, which are nothing like so formalized, were expected to act automatically. Rather they seem to strain towards an end, an unachieved completeness of mutual understanding between man and beast in and through the holy rock.

If the hunting of game is preceded and followed by a rite, it follows that the hunt itself is in some sense a part of the rite. The culmination of entreaty for the betrayal and death of the beast is the

[1] L. Adam, *Primitive Art*, 1949 ed., p. 176.

death itself, followed in due course by the
feast, in which the power or powers who
assisted victory might presumably claim a
share. In the course of time, as we know,
some of the beasts represented in the
caves, the bulls and their cows, the horses,
boars and sows, and other beasts whose
relationships with man must have been of
a similar kind, goats, sheep, dogs, and
cats, came to be by slow stages domesti-
cated. They lost some of their fear of man
and entered into a permanent relationship with him. We misunderstand the
early stages of this relationship if we
think of the typical cow or sheep of the
last two centuries, a placid beast in a
fertile meadow, fattened for milking,
shearing, and slaughter. We shall understand it better if we think of the shepherd and goatherd following his flock
across the hills, attending to all their
needs, but only rarely feeding on their
precious flesh. The relationship between a
Bantu tribe and their cattle is not now
economic. Men must have cattle to be
men. The Indian tends his cattle, but
eats no meat at all. He makes some use of

them for ploughing and dunging. He may use their hides and hoofs when they have died in venerable old age. But to eat them is out of the question. This is an extreme case, the result of a peculiar development in the Indian climate. But it illustrates the appropriateness of an ancient pyramid text: "Well tended are men, the cattle of god."[1] For many centuries in many cultures men have laboured for cattle, more than cattle for men. The beast, especially the bull, has been regarded as in some important respect superior in strength and sanctity to his herdmen.

The ritual slaying of beasts in sacrifice must be understood in this context. It is best considered as a development of the ritual hunt. An intermediate stage survives in the bullfight, of which we have evidence from incised cups found among Minoan remains in Crete, and in the amphitheatre at Cnossos.[2] Several other amphitheatres on other sites in

---

[1] H. Frankfort, *Kingship and the Gods*, Chicago, 1946, pp. 163, 182.

[2] See G. Levy, *The Gate of Horn*, 1947, pp. 229, 249, 295.

Europe and Asia were probably used for similar games. It is a mistake to regard the animal victim as a substitute for a king or a man. This mistake, which is still widely current, arises first of all from a misunderstanding of some traditions as to the origin of sacrifice. Every ritual tends to develop a myth to explain its origins, which is often recited in the course of the ceremonies. At a later stage speculation interprets both myth and ritual in accordance with theological ideas. But the action is primary, the myth secondary. The theological explanation may throw a powerful light on the motives which lead men to continue the performance of the ritual and the recitation of the myth. As these motives remain the same through many changes in the shape of the liturgy and the details of the story, the theology of sacrifice does throw some light on its nature and origins. So does the myth, if we regard it as a dramatization of human motive. But it is a mistake to take it as traditional evidence for the origin of the ritual.

A great deal of modern research into

the origins of the idea of sacrifice has been dominated by a theme which found its most complete expression in Freud's *Totem and Taboo*. Yet I think it was in the air before Freud. It had too much influence on Frazer, who knew nothing of Freud when he embarked on *The Golden Bough*. This is the idea of a primitive clan dominated by an old man, whose many wives will be commandeered in the end by the most persistent and valiant of his sons. He kills his sons as long as he can to avoid this catastrophe, but is in the end killed and eaten by his victorious successor, who thereby acquires his power. In this view, which finds some support in such myths as the story of Cronos, who ate all his children except his son and successor Zeus, we all want to kill father and marry mother, but we relieve ourselves of this incestuous desire by killing a bull or a goat instead. We are all afraid of our firstborn sons, who immediately become our potential rivals, and sacrifice lambs to avoid eating the baby. I find this very unconvincing. It seems to me to reveal a modern, not an ancient tension between the older and the younger generation, something that arises out of rapid revolutions in science and thinking, and the Victorian idea of progress. Chiefs indeed are sometimes sacrificed when they have passed their prime, but we generally find that in such cases they have acquired ritual functions which are essential to the welfare of the tribe, and yet so very complicated that they cannot be conducted with accuracy by an old man. Either the priest-king must be surrounded with a sufficient supply of servants to keep his life regulated to perfection, like the life of a Pharaoh in Egypt and of the Mikado in Japan, or he must die the death when his personal potency is exhausted. So far as I know no Pharaoh of Egypt was sacrificed, but the imitation of Pharaoh in smaller communities, European and African, might easily lead to a situation in which death was the only door out. It is significant that Frazer's modern examples of sacrificed kings are in the Nile and Congo valleys. He made the mistake of seeing the origins of the Egyptian monarchy in central Africa. It is far more likely that the Shilluk king of Fashoda,[1] like the Kabaka of Uganda and the Lion-king of Ethiopia, is an imitation of Pharaoh, who lacks resources to keep his ritual potency unimpaired.

Other examples of sacrificed kings would seem to be cases of deliberate and voluntary surrender to death where the ordinary means of appeasing wrath had failed. In a society increasingly conscious of a certain superiority of man over beast, a beast victim will appear increasingly insufficient. If the priests cannot appease the divine power by ordinary means, a trump card must be played, the king's daughter, his eldest son, or the king himself. But this does not mean that the bull in ordinary years is the king's substitute. Even the custom of killing a substitute king, arrayed in regalia for the occasion, is much more likely to have arisen out of such emergencies in a developed civilization, than to be a survival of earlier days before animal sacrifice.

If we look for a time before the slaying

[1] See *The Dying God*, 1911 ed., pp. 17–28.

of beasts was in any way ritualized, we must seek it in a very remote period. It may be that the rites associated with the death of animals are in some way derived from the funeral rites of human beings, of which the first scanty evidence[1] goes back for thousands of years before the cave paintings. Of these rites we know next to nothing. We can only divine their nature from the presence of cup-like depressions beside graves, and traces of red ochre in human remains. I can see no evidence to connect the first funerals with ritual murder. The primacy of the female image in the Aurignacian statuettes and the bas-relief at Laussel, which appear to represent one and the same divinity, suggests an opposite pattern of society to that conceived by Frazer and Freud. According to Robert Graves[2] the women stayed by the fire, tended plants in the first gardens, stirred the cooking-pot, built the wall. The hearth belonged to them and to their children. They lured strange young men to their fires and married them to their

[1] See Levy, *op. cit.*, p. 6.
[2] In *The White Goddess*.

daughters, but drove away their hunter sons to find other brides in other settlements.

This version of the story is no more adequate to all the evidence than Freud's in *Totem and Taboo*, but it is based on two facts, the long roots of exogamy, and the common custom of matrilineal succession, which does not always imply matriarchal rule. Exogamy may be better explained by the danger of conflicts between males, and matrilineal succession by the fact that maternity is certain, paternity problematical, while hearth and home are common to the clan. But it is not surprising that communities who reckon descent in this fashion, and look for new men from elsewhere, should think of the earth as a mother and speed the dead of man and beast to her hearth and fire, that their life might help her to bring forth new children every year.

If so, we may suppose that sacrifice begins with the necessary death of a victim whose flesh and blood are required to renew the fertility of the soil and the fecundity of the tribe and of the herd.

At first he will be a hunted beast or a hunter killed by a beast, but soon a selected victim. The Ainu in northern Japan, who live largely on bear, tend a bear cub every year in their houses, and kill him solemnly after many apologies, not to the particular bear only, but to the whole race of bears.[1] That the primitive hunter wished his beasts to increase and multiply is clear from his concern not only with their death, but with their reproduction. Mating and dying are depicted in the same way on the same walls in the Pyrenean caves. This concern continues in the pastoral period, when the shepherd and goatherd tend their flocks through parturition, and slay them only with ceremony and restraint. The ceremony implies that the victim is an object of reverence, and that his death takes place according to a pre-ordained order, by some kind of divine permission. If ritual is older than myth, and myth than theology, sacrifice of some kind may be older than the idea of a personal god or goddess. Funeral rites for men and beasts,

[1] Jane Harrison, *Ancient Art and Ritual*, 1913, pp. 92–8.

for the doomed and the dying, are first of all addressed to them and to the world of death, whither they go and cannot return. But death is a kind of marriage, with the underworld and the earth. If the mating and dying of beasts are related, as in art, so in life, so are death, marriage, and birth in men. When the Lamb has been slain "the marriage of the Lamb is come, and his bride has made herself ready." The bride of the Lamb is the heaven above, and the earth beneath, and the water under the earth, the circle around everything, the great river and the great worm.

# Chapter II: The Divine Victim

THE first divine images which have survived are of women, of great beasts, and of half-human, half-animal monsters. All the Egyptian gods are beasts, birds, or monsters except the three, Osiris, Isis, and Horus, who clearly belong to the development of irrigation and the kingdom. Even Isis has cow's horns, and Horus often bears the form of a falcon. The God of Israel was represented in the form of a bull in the shrines of Bethel and Dan.[1] In the temple at Jerusalem his seat was between the cherubim,[2] great winged monsters, or he might be conceived as standing over the brazen sea, which stood upon twelve oxen.[3] His Ark was drawn by two heifers[4] from Ekron to Beth-Shemesh. If, as seems very

---

[1] I Kings 12, v. 28, cf. Exodus 32, vv. 4, 24. But some would hold that the single bulls at Bethel and Dan were his thrones, like the many oxen in the temple at Jerusalem.
[2] I Samuel 4, v. 4.    [3] I Kings 7, v. 25.    [4] I Samuel 6.

likely, the story of Noah's Ark reflects a rain-making ritual, images of beasts were taken in and out of it at some festival for the increase of flocks and fruits. This kind of imagery persists in Christianity, not only in the visions of the Apocalypse, but for instance at S. Apollinare in Classe at Ravenna, where the transfigured Christ is a huge cross, and all the apostles are sheep, and in the oratory of S. Andrew in the archbishop's palace there where four great monsters circle round the chi-rho diagram in the circuit of heaven.

The first portrayal of God or the gods in the form of a human male appears to have arisen through the metamorphosis of wild monsters in the wilderness. Where most vegetation is wild, in fields between the forests, the spirit of the corn continues to be a beast. But where the wilderness is barren, and fields and gardens in need of rain, he may be portrayed in human form as a girl or a young man. It is important in considering the growth of this custom to remember how ritual precedes myth. At the end of summer in

Greece and western Asia, when the garden is dry and bare, the dead vegetation is cleared away, burnt up or dug in. Men and women cry for rain before the rains come; they weep and the sky weeps with them. Rainy days are a sad time, even for those who desire rain. The goddess and the women are mourning someone, but whom? The stock indeed will have to be reduced; bulls and lambs will soon be sacrificed. But it may be inadequate to say that the goddess mourns for her doomed bull calf, her kid or her ram. Rather she mourns her lover, her husband, or her child, son or daughter. Why did he die or disappear? In some myths she herself may be directly responsible, like a girl who tells her lover to fight a boar for her, but cries when he falls in combat. The goddess, unlike a girl, can revive her lover to reign with her among the dead, and send forth shoots of spring from under the earth. But frequently the myth becomes more complicated. Aphrodite or Astarte found Adonis or Tammuz, a wonderful babe who was born from a split tree. She put him out to nurse with her underworld aspect, who insisted on keeping him half or a third of the year. This is one myth of the origin of winter. In another, Demeter's daughter was kidnapped by Hades, who let her go back to her mother at regular intervals. But Persephone in other myths appears to be queen of the dead in her own right. She is really another, perhaps an older aspect of her mother Demeter, lady of life and death. The story is told to explain mourning and weeping in autumn, but it implies conflict and tension between life and death in Nature. So does the story of Osiris, murdered by his brother Set, sought and found by his wife, the great mother Isis. Here again the end of conflict is a kind of compromise. Osiris reigns in the land of the dead, over the great majority in Egyptian eyes, but the land of the living, Upper and Lower Egypt, is divided between Set and Horus, the avenging son. So in some fashion harmony is restored, to be broken again and mended year by year.

Agriculture intensifies this conflict, for

the ploughing and irrigation of fields involves more violence to Nature than gardening or hunting. Ploughing and sowing must have their own ritual rehearsal, like hunting in the caves, and gardening in the gardens of Adonis, tiny boxes filled with earth, sown and watered every year at the first rains, to sprout quickly and die quickly. No doubt some of these hunting and gardening rites had their own songs, and some of the songs were songs of origins. Agricultural creation myths often include an element that seems to come down from a time when the world seemed like an egg, laid by a great bird, when all created things issued from the body of a goddess or a god. The new element that comes in with the ploughed field is the idea that the world was made or founded, like a new city, a new settlement, fenced by a wall from the desert, provided from the first with institutions, including prescribed rituals and a calendar of good and evil days. In agricultural creation myths a god or gods do battle with the elements of chaos, the beasts and satyrs of the wilderness, and in

44

some sense with Nature herself. Marduk defeats Tiamat, and carves her body asunder into earth and sky. He divides the waters from the waters, ploughs the earth as a field, separating land from sea, raising hills like ridges between rivers. At the end of his long labours he will marry Tiamat in another aspect, as Ishtar-Zaparit who waits for him on her holy mountain. But as agriculture and politics, city life and warfare develop, Ishtar-Astarte plays a more passive part. In some early myths she visits the underworld to bring the god back, and suffers a progressive stripping of her garments until she find her lord and release him from the bonds of her deathly counterpart.[1] But in the developed ritual of the Babylonian Akitu festival her part is merely to mourn for him. His son and successor Nabu must dig him out of the mountain to join his bride on her bed on top of the ziggurat.[2]

In this agricultural ritual the god is still sacrificed, but the identity of god and

[1] See S. N. Kramer, *Sumerian Mythology*, Philadelphia, 1944, pp. 83–96.

[2] See Frankfort, *op. cit.*, chapter 22.

victim is in a measure loosened. The slain beasts sustain the god in his work of recreation, but the god is no more immanent in his beasts than he is in his people, who suffer with him in his burial and feast with him at his marriage. The death of a substitute king, which sometimes formed part of the rite, seems to indicate a sense that the participation of the realm in the god's death and resurrection must be as complete as possible. The people's share in the divine marriage was accomplished through ritual embraces between male members of the human community and dedicated representatives of his divine bride. But the gap between god and Nature is widening, not closing, despite ecstatic efforts. The sun and stars are now of supreme importance. The determination of destinies, the most important part of the yearly ritual, signifies the establishment of a calendar, the publication, as we might say, of an official almanack in which works and days are determined for the whole year for all classes. This goes by the positions of sun and stars. They matter much more than the beasts, who are now in the service of man to bear his burdens. Man's control over beasts and crops now depends on his ability to keep in step with the movements of heavenly powers. They encounter no resistance in their regular passage through the sky, but he must struggle with recalcitrant elements, mud and marsh and weeds and satyrs of the wilderness. Death is hostile to life as she was not when the mother of the dead and the living was all one, when the death of men and beasts availed to ensure her fertility, for she is winter and the wilderness, the darkness of chaos, the power of the enemy. Monism gives place to a kind of dualism.

Agriculture everywhere intensified men's sense of evil, by drawing a sharper distinction between plants and weeds. This hardly exists in the forest and mountain pasture. In the garden there are intermediate stages, but the ploughed field is made for a crop. Its wildness and wet are due either to the infirmity of the soil or to the activity of an evil interloper. Persian religion saw the sources of evil in hostile spirits, rebellious evil wills, not in the matter of creation, though part of that matter had been infected by demonic agency. The Persians may not have been certain whether Ahriman was a rebellious angel, or an elementary and original principle. They were sure that he was an evil will, and that their god struggled with him, and suffered with them, to maintain the life of creation against decay, deceit, and illusion.

Another and opposite estimate of creation is implied in nearly all Indian and a great deal of Greek philosophy and religion. It is that creation itself is a fall of spirit into matter, that perfect being is torn, divided, and concealed in forms of miserable clay. True being is above and beyond this world in the land of stars, beyond the stars in a land of perfect forms, or beyond all forms in a union that passes all understanding. Matter is a clog on spirit; mud and marsh resist the order imposed by the plough and the stars. This earth is the lowest, the meanest, the most fallen of a succession of descending planes or spheres.

The suffering god in the Orphic myth has been captured and devoured by Titans. The human race was made from his remains, mingled with theirs.[1] The god can only escape to the outer and upper world through us, if we will endure a long discipline of purification, whereby we may release him in us from the labyrinth of birth and death. Much of the material of this mythology goes back to the earliest times. It is a new explanation of rites intended to imitate and encourage generation, the birth and growth of children, beasts, and corn. But these rites are now interpreted as pointing to regeneration, to some mystic means whereby we may not achieve but avoid rebirth, establish ourselves permanently in another world, a heavenly world which is not this, is free from the trammels of flesh and the clogs of clay. In this view of the world suffering is not voluntary, but necessary. Death and birth, in ourselves and the beasts, are burdens inflicted upon us by our sad condition.

[1] See Jane Harrison, *Prolegomena to the Study of Greek Religion*, 1903, pp. 479–97, Levy, *op. cit.*, pp. 273–99.

Hinayana Buddhism, which seems to be a kind of Indian cousin to Orphism, accepts something like this view of the matter. But in the later Buddhism, the Mahayana, it is relieved by the idea of a heavenly being, who for our sake has accepted suffering, to help us on the way out of our earthly prison. This is very near, not indeed to orthodox Christianity, but to the semi-Christianity of Gnosticism and Docetism.[1] The idea of a willing sacrifice at the heart of creation, of the pain and travail of God for creatures, is indeed acknowledged, but not the possibility that the world itself, the world of birth, labour, and death, is God's manifestation, the place of His life, death, and resurrection. "The Lamb of God that taketh away the sins of the world" is nearer to the beasts of Lascaux and Altamira, who are willed and will to suffer with the hunter, than He is to the dying gods of agricultural ritual, to Adonis, Osiris, and Marduk, who battle through the mud and are buried by a

[1] See H. de Lubac, *Aspects of Buddhism*, Eng. trans., 1953, pp. 118–19.

recalcitrant element. Yet He himself is slain by human sin, not only the sin of the chosen people, who sincerely believed that in killing Him they were averting blasphemy, and vindicating the divine unity, but by the carelessness, the casualness of Herod and Pilate, the inertia, the easy-going drift, that agricultural religion rightly sees as the road to chaos and the wilderness.

Humanly speaking, laying aside for the moment the idea of a divine vocation, the significance of Israel lies in the protest of a people who conserve pre-agricultural traditions against the tyranny of agricultural ritual. It is important to distinguish between objections to the sacred marriage of Baal and Astarte, and the rejection of all images of God. I cannot believe that the war between Elijah and Jezebel was merely a matter of nationalism, or of a kind of rainmaking competition between two types of ritual. The whole point of the story is that rain cannot be obtained by ritual, but only at the will of a God, revealed through a prophet who is a helpless instrument of divinity, often frustrated, disappointed, and despairing. The significance of Jezebel, on the other hand, lies in her witchcraft and her whoredoms.[1] The image of a divine bride, with hair tired, looking out of the window, has been found among the scattered fragments of her ivory house.[2] So tradition imagined Jezebel herself in her hour of death. She was Astarte's representative. Yet Jehu, who caused her death in the revolution stirred up by Elisha's preaching, venerated the bulls at Dan and Bethel, to the disgust of the Judean author of the Book of Kings. I see no evidence that Elijah or Elisha, or any other northern reformer, raised objections to these bull images until Hosea[3] made a criticism of calves that implies some criticism of all sacrifices.

Here lies the real difficulty. The later Israelites sought to retain sacrificial institutions, and even agricultural festivals, but they did all that they possibly could to root these rituals in divine commands given in the heroic age of wilderness

[1] II Kings 9, v. 22.
[2] Now in the Palestine Museum, Jerusalem (Jordan).
13, v. 2.

wandering, before the settlement in Canaan. They divided the God from the victim, and made of every offering an act of homage, in obedience to the written law, to the revealed Will. In their myth (if we may use the word without prejudice of any tale told to explain a ritual) the suffering God is replaced by His suffering people, who at His command, and by His supernatural aid, descend to the prison of Egypt, but rise again through storm, plague, and flood, divide the waters from the waters in the Red Sea and the river Jordan, and pass in to possess the land. In their suffering He is with them. Something is left of the divine suffering, for, "In all their afflictions He was afflicted, and the angel of His presence saved them."[1] But his people, not Himself, endure humiliation. In the first chapter of the myth, in the creation story of Genesis, almost everything is eliminated that implies a struggle to create. "He spake, and it was done. He commanded, and it stood fast." He is above and beyond the process.

The strongest proof of the divine

[1] Isaiah 63, v. 9.

vocation of Israel lies in their extraordinary success in eliminating images of God without losing their sense that He was and is Someone, the living God who acts, not a divinity dispersed behind and within the infinite variety of earthly and heavenly things. This depends at least in part on their strong belief that their own mythology was rooted in history, that He had called them out of Egypt to possess the land, that He had brought them back from Babylon, and had a further purpose for them. The remembrance of His deeds enabled them to dispense with His image in any form, even the Ark, a shape inherited, as we may conjecture, from the age of caves and the Great Mother.[1] The Israelites travelled away from any image of the impassible, human or animal, male or female. Only vestiges remain through the necessities of language. Even the divine name was seldom spoken, and written only with the utmost care and deliberation.

This is more than an achievement. It is

[1] *Supra*, p. 41.

a gift, and can only be understood as a gift. But such a gift implies limitations. The Jews were not philosophers. To speak of their religious genius is beside the point, for nothing in their religious practice was original or peculiar to themselves. What is truly distinctive about them is their refusal to acknowledge a manifestation of divine power either in the sacrificed victim or in the priest who manipulated the offering. Other peoples performed sacrifices largely, though not entirely, to obtain auspices, some sign of favour or displeasure in the sacrificed flesh. The Jews did so in obedience to the revealed word. Their rituals developed by limitation, to special times and a special place, which became more and more inaccessible to the greater part of the nation, not only in the dispersion, but in the scattered towns and villages of Palestine. The sacrificial side of Judaism gradually became residuary. What mattered was the observance of the whole law, for this was possible anywhere and everywhere.

The temple at Jerusalem might be remote and inaccessible, but in the Jewish home all life is ritual. The destruction of Jerusalem was not a disaster for developed Judaism, but rather the fulfilment of a process which began with the decay and demolition of the High Places. Those who rejected Christ went on their way to create a religious way of life entirely purged from animal sacrifices except for the single survival, the Passover feast. Those who accepted Him saw the veil of the Temple rent from top to bottom, the wall of partition broken down. They inherited from Israel the gift of faith in a transcendent God, but recovered what the Jews had lost, and the Gentiles in their own ways retained, a sense of the immanent presence of the divine victim sacrificed, once for all in one historical event, represented and remembered in the eucharistic act.

In our right reaction against some modern interpretations of Christianity as the last and greatest of the Hellenistic mysteries, parallel to Mahayana Buddhism

in the farther East, we may not diminish
the scandal of the cross to the rabbinical
mind. S. Paul's Jewish critics, most of
whom wanted to be Christians, were
offended at the thought of justification
by faith in the death and resurrection of
Christ, of our burial with Him, that we
may be partakers of His resurrection,
because this seemed to them a surrender
to paganism, in that very aspect which
Jewry had most steadfastly resisted, the
actual identification of the worshipper
with his god. So it seemed, not only to
Jewish critics, but to some of S. Paul's
disciples in the Gentile churches. Unless
we believe that Gnosticism was a religion
already existing, which infiltrated into the
Christian churches (and of this there is no
clear evidence), we must regard Gnosis as
an interpretation of the Christian mystery
in pagan terms, which in a pagan world
had every chance of success. How that
success was averted we still have to consider, but we shall underestimate the
danger unless we realize how like the
Gospel looked to popular paganism, not
only in the eyes of orthodox Judaism.

57

# LAMB TO THE SLAUGHTER

Christ crucified on the cross was "to the Jews a stumbling-block, and to the Greeks foolishness," but familiar foolishness, another oriental mystery religion whose precise difference from all the rest did not at first seem to deserve investigation.

# Chapter III: *The Lamb of God*

HOW do we explain correspondences between sacrificial rituals and the life and death of Christ? This is in no way a new question. The idea of Christ's death as a sacrifice, of Christ as our Passover, the Lamb of God that taketh away the sins of the world, is deeply embedded in the text of the New Testament. Much of the older exegesis of the Old Testament, patristic, medieval, and post-Reformation, was concerned to establish exact correspondences between Calvary and some or all of the Levitical sacrifices. In modern times the same search for parallels, extended over a wider field, has become the occasion of destructive criticism. It has been argued that the passion of Christ and His resurrection are the last and most substantial version of the myth of Osiris and Tammuz, a tale told to explain Christian baptism, the annual Pasch, and the weekly or daily feast on the Body and Blood of Christ.

The theory that the life of Christ is a myth pure and simple has had few upholders for many years. But a modified version of the same theory is probably held by most non-Christians who have reflected seriously on the early history of Christianity, and is entertained by many whose general attitude to the Christian religion is more positive than negative. We may hold various opinions about Professor Toynbee's general thesis in *The Study of History*, and about the usefulness of his kind of inquiry into the pattern of historical development, but none of us can gainsay his learning, and few will write him off as a wild man. He is careful with his qualifications; his underlying scale of values seems to many people conventional rather than original; and his more recent publications have been criticized by historians as excessively preoccupied with religion and the Christian religion. At the end of his sixth volume, published in 1939, he includes a whole series of annexes, extending over nearly two hundred pages, nearly all concerned with "correspondences between the story of Jesus and the stories of certain Hellenic saviours." These are summarized in a series of tables, ten in all, covering twelve pages.

His conclusion is that several accounts of real historical figures, including Jesus Christ, have been coloured and heightened by conscious or unconscious assimilation to a later form of the legend of Heracles, and to the older myth of the dying and rising god. Some correspondences may be due to the deliberate imitation of gods and heroes by such historical characters as King Cleomenes III of Sparta or Gaius Gracchus. Some may be simply fortuitous, but a large number point to the compelling influence of myth upon the biographer. In the case of the Gospels, where parallels, even in small details, with pagan legend are too numerous to be the result of mere chance, the easiest explanation is to be found in the assimilation of history to current folklore and myth.

Nearly all the professor's parallels are taken from literature which might be familiar to Christian readers in the second half of the first century A.D. A few are from Buddhist texts of the same period, which seem to have absorbed material from Greek and Syriac legend. I myself think Professor Toynbee too eager to see analogies, not only in the lives of heroes, but in the sequence of historical events. His whole view of history compels him to reduce the individual to a symbol of the *zeitgeist*, and to translate biography into sociology dramatized. But in this he is very representative. We cannot afford to ignore his comment.

Three types of correspondence between the New Testament and ancient ritual seem especially significant. The first is the simplest, the most straightforward, and the easiest to explain to the satisfaction of the agnostic and the Christian. Christ slain at the Passover, is identified in the Gospels and the Epistles with the Paschal lamb, "the Lamb of God that taketh away the sins of the world," "Christ our Passover," "a lamb as it had been slain." If, as seems very probable, Hebrew poetry lies behind the account of our Lord's birth as given in

S. Luke's Gospel, we may reasonably suppose that one of its motives was the worship of a young child in a beast's manger by those who tend and care for young lambs. "He was led as a sheep to the slaughter." He was also hunted, through hairbreadth escapes: "Foxes have holes, birds of the air have nests, but the Son of Man hath not where to lay his head." In the end He was caught and crucified.

The second is the parallel with Tammuz, Adonis, Dionysus, and Osiris. Our Lord foretold his sacrificial death. He was slain at a spring feast, in which He himself identified His Body and Blood with bread and wine. He was crowned with thorns in mockery, clad in a purple robe, and crucified on a tree. His body was prepared for burial by a woman bearing his mother's name, Mary. In S. John's Gospel: "There stood by the cross of Jesus His mother and His mother's sister, Mary the wife of Cleopas, and Mary Magdalene," or in S. Mark: "There were also women beholding from afar, among whom were both Mary Magdalene, and

Mary the mother of James the less and of Joses, and Salome." These three "beheld where He was laid." "And very early on the first day of the week, they came to the tomb when the sun was risen." "He appeared first to Mary Magdalene." The number of Marys does not trouble us, for the name has become so excessively common. No doubt the name of Moses' sister Miriam was common among the Jews of our Lord's time. And yet it would seem that all the evangelists saw some significant identity between the Marys. Are they all Isis, Ishtar, Astarte?

The third is the royal entry of the divine king into Jerusalem, the cleansing of the Temple and the solemn determination of destinies for the city and the world before the arrest and the crucifixion. Christ comes to the holy city as the Son of Man, foretelling His own return. He rises to the right hand of the Father at the end of the story, to descend again at another end, beyond history. He does battle with chaos in the wilderness, and in the cleansing of the demoniacs. He "beheld Satan as lightning fallen from heaven." Not indeed in the gospels, but in a very early stratum of Christian literature he has "preached to the spirits in prison,"[1] and harrowed hell like Heracles.

The first set of parallels involves the minimum of difficulty. If Christ was killed at Passover time the Passover must inevitably become for His disciples the annual commemoration of His death and passion. To Gentile Christians, excluded from Paschal rites, He was and is their only Paschal Lamb. His sacramental feast, renewed not annually but often, super-seded Passover and carried with it the Paschal imagery of deliverance from Egypt. If we allow any poetry at all in the Gospel story we can admit the intrusion of Paschal themes into the narrative of the nativity.

The third set of correspondences con-ceals significant differences. In the story of Christ the battle with chaos is always a battle with spiritual evil. The enemy is not earth and mud, but Satan and his myrmidons. The mythical background, if we allow the use of such terms, is Jewish,

[1] I Peter 3, v. 19; cf. 4, v. 6.

perhaps ultimately Persian, but not Greek or Babylonian.

The second is, I believe, the real crux. We might admit the lamb imagery to be embroidery. We all to some extent demythologize the evangelical account of demoniac possession, allowing for the probability that some recognized kinds of mental disease played a part in such cases. But if we believe that the bodily resurrection, and the words "This is my Body . . . This is my Blood" at the Last Supper are literary infiltrations into historical sources, we must hold that the entire story has been transmuted at the most critical point from history into myth.

We cannot gainsay the fact that if the myth-making imagination has been at work, this is exactly the point at which it might be expected to operate, to justify a sacrificial explanation of the eucharistic rite, and to hold forth to initiated believers the certainty of union after death with the risen Christ. Nor can we deny that baptism and the eucharist are dominant themes in all four Gospels. Present tendencies in New Testament studies, among the form critics and the typologists, agree in pointing to the influence of practical and liturgical problems in the Christian community upon the form and content of the story.

I believe the answer to the problem of history must be found outside the text of the Gospels, in a consideration of the Epistles, which are better historical material than the Gospels themselves, because of their occasional character, their loose construction, their lack of literary finish and form. If we had no evidence except the Epistles we should still be sure that Paul of Tarsus was an historical character, in some tension with other leaders of the Christian community on such points as the obligation of the Levitical law, and the future relations of Christianity to organized Jewry. But in all the documents that may be used to illustrate this tension, including one, the Epistle of S. James, which seems to come from the other side of the controversy, there is not the smallest sign of disagreement about the fact of the resurrection, and its centrality in Christian preaching, or about the customary observance of the eucharistic feast. We may indeed allow for the possibility of differences on the interpretation of the death of Christ, and on the significance of the eucharist, perhaps also on the manner of its celebration, but the preaching of the resurrection and the breaking of bread is common to all parties. Unless S. Paul's Epistles, including Galatians and Corinthians, are a literary construction, we have evidence for the Last Supper and the resurrection older than the Synoptic Gospels, transmitted by S. Paul to his disciples on the authority of the first Christians.

If the eucharist and the resurrection were part of the datum of tradition for all Christians before S. Paul's preaching, the other less important parallels with spring myths in all the Gospels are easily explained. It would be absurd to suppose S. Mark and S. John ignorant of the general lines of fertility ritual in the Near East. They knew very much more about it than any of us. As Jews, and as contemporaries of the decay of pagan religion, they probably disliked it very intensely, but they were neither ignorant nor innocent. They were aware of parallels between their story and the myths, probably already exploited by Jews for polemical purposes. In the next century at any rate the Jews were to the fore in accusing Christians of ritual murder, a charge which clearly implies an interpretation of baptism and the eucharist in terms of pagan myth. The Evangelists all refer to their Hebrew sources. Sometimes, it has been suggested, they modified details to suit prophecies. They never say "as Heracles did." They may have been completely unaware of some scenes and properties from pagan myth that had become part of their mental background. But they could hardly avoid using Hellenistic literary images. A modern parallel may here be helpful. Some of Mr. Eliot's allusions to other poetry are conscious and deliberate, like the Evangelists' quotations from the prophets. A great many were unconscious, though he will not deny, when the fact is brought to his notice, that such and such a line or passage was part of his reading, and may have been at the back of his mind at the time. I myself should be inclined to interpret in this way the tendency of all the Evangelists to fuse the women who followed Christ into one woman, His mother and His Church, the bride of the Lamb, who plays the part of Demeter and Isis, Astarte and Ishtar, in the Christian mystery drama.

The problem remains, how much concern had the Evangelists with what we call history? Modern critical discussions of the New Testament in recent years do not greatly help in this inquiry. It is not enough to insist that the Evangelists must have been Jews, and that their primary material is the Old Testament, for on all accounts they were Jews writing in Greek, in the Hellenistic world, for Jews and Gentiles in Greek cities and Asiatic villages. We may, however, compare their concerns with those of others, at work among their contemporaries, who conceived the kind of stories embodied a little later in apocryphal acts and apocryphal gospels. In the New Testament itself[1] we can see some traces of

[1] e.g. I John 4, v. 2; cf. *ibid.* 1, v. 1.

polemic against another version of the
story of Jesus, which is pure myth, without a virgin birth, because a god cannot
be born of a woman, without a resurrection, because there can be no crucifixion.
An immortal god cannot die.

The Gnostic saviour, Christ or Buddha,
is a stranger god come down from the
back of beyond to lead his people through
the labyrinth of the heavens, behind the
circuits of celestial spheres, to an unde-
filed happy land. To keep his secrets
pure he must escape all material defile-
ment, and therefore his coming must be
entirely miraculous. There is a very strik-
ing resemblance between Mahayana tales
of the childhood of Buddha and the
*Protevangelion* of James on the infancy of
the Blessed Virgin and of Christ.[1]

If the strife were between a myth with
a virgin birth, a shameful death, and a
bodily resurrection, and another myth
about an apparition, the odds would seem
to be in favour of Docetism. Apparitions
were common form in the Near East, and

[1] For Buddhist and Christian Docetism see especially
H. de Lubac, *op. cit.*, pp. 115–19.

a great deal of later Greek philosophy approved the Gnostic view of the body. A useful list of familiar quotations will be found in Clement of Alexandria's tract on marriage, lately translated by Mr. Henry Chadwick, who points out in his introduction that S. Jerome's polemic on the same subject, so often quoted as an extreme instance of ascetic depreciation of the flesh, is taken wholesale, without acknowledgement, from the pagan Porphyry's summary of the lessons of Greek philosophy.[1]

The Achilles' heel of Christian Gnosticism was a compromise between myth and history. Gnostics fastened on the person of Christ, and made him their saviour instead of Dionysus, Heracles, or Orpheus. The need of a new god was acute, for all the old myths were worn out. Marcion, who of all the Gnostics had the keenest intelligence, seems to have shrewdly seen the main difficulties on both sides. The four Gospels contained crudities abhorrent to a sensitive intelli-

[1] *Alexandrian Christianity*, translations by J. E. L. Oulton and H. Chadwick, 1954, p. 37.

gence, and the Old Testament was much worse. On the other hand the romances of his contemporaries, their mystical interpretations of the Hebrew prophets, and fantastic accounts of the pre-existent Christ, could not satisfy a real thirst for more knowledge of His life. Marcion put into circulation, not a complete and rounded myth, but an expurgated version of the New Testament, consisting of the Gospel of S. Luke, without the infancy narratives, and some of S. Paul's Epistles, without their rabbinical references, and so revised as to appear consistently opposed to the old law.

Marcion came nearer to success than the other Gnostics. His church persisted for some centuries. His strength and weakness underlines the real strength of the Catholic churches. The churches in the second century were not served by a galaxy of brilliant thinkers. In their choice of canonical books they were indeed assisted by the Holy Spirit, but if we look at their task on the human level, as they did, it seems unlikely that they could use the tools of theological analysis.

They did not reject the Epistle of Barnabas because of its extravagant allegories, for they did such things themselves. To a great extent they shared the common Greek view of the physical body, and therefore much in the rejected gospels of the infancy of Christ, and in the apocryphal acts of the Apostles would not shock them as it shocks us. On the other hand they had evidence of the Apostolic origin of books, in actual manuscripts and in recollections not now recorded, but then common knowledge.

Marcion and the Catholic churches were in competition to produce an authentic collection. His was the more consistent, but theirs was the more complete. They omitted such orthodox books as the First Epistle of Clement, and the Ignatian Letters, because they did not come from Apostles. They questioned the Epistle to the Hebrews, because they were not sure of its authorship. Here and there by their own standards they made a mistake, over the Second Epistle of S. Peter (which long remained among the disputed books), and the Pastoral Epistles, which probably contain fragments from authentic personal letters of S. Paul, preserved (like the Epistle to Philemon), but edited for general circulation. They did not try to smooth down what looks like flat contradiction between the Epistle of S. James and S. Paul's Epistles to the Galatians and the Romans. They won the victory over Marcion, not because they produced better mythology, but because they convicted him of cooking his history.

The four Gospels are works of literature containing historical matter, some of it recalcitrant to literary treatment, all of it bent to a pattern of presentation, like a mosaic or a Byzantine icon. But there are four of them. The churches declined to select one, like Marcion, or to weave them into consistency, like Tatian. History in our sense was yet to be born, but the presence of a sense of history is proved by the preservation of illustrative documents interesting not for their literary form, but simply as records, not only of the Apostolic Epistles, but of such letters as those of Ignatius, Polycarp, and the martyrs of Lyons. No doubt they were used to support exhortations, not for their eloquence but as examples.

If the Last Supper and the resurrection are history, not mythology, the sacrificial character of our Lord's death stands out clearly, on the evidence of the Epistles, even if He did not say in the words of the Gospels that: "The Son of Man came not to be ministered unto, but to minister, and to give His life as a ransom for many." This is probable, but not necessary, if He died at the spring feast and rose again like the corn god, to make Himself known to His disciples in the breaking of bread. These facts, if they were facts, were themselves enough to defeat the Orphic and Gnostical interpretations of ancient ritual, and to substitute a fulfilment of prophecy, making sense, not only of the Old Testament, but of the age-old mystery of fertility. The glory of the Christian gospel lay in its claim to be history. In this it did satisfy a religious need, by the instant proclamation that here "types and shadows have their ending," that the body is not a prison but a temple prepared for resurrection.

The resurrection of the body depends on the empty tomb, not the empty tomb on a myth of resurrection. If we consider the difficulty of believing a resurrection of the flesh against the grain of later Greek and oriental civilization, it seems clear that the Easter story could never be, in that age at least, a creation of myth. It began a new myth, a human historical version of myths of the rising corn. This year, every year, every week, every morning, Christ is risen.

# Chapter IV: The Paschal Mystery

CHRISTIANITY began as a Jewish sect, which acknowledged Jesus Christ as the Messiah risen from the dead, and admitted Gentile converts to full membership by baptism without circumcision. Christians had a form of synagogue service based on traditional models, and a common meal which included the breaking of bread and communion in the cup of blessing. Baptism was administered without much preparation in New Testament times. But before the beginning of the second century the church had become predominantly Gentile, not Jewish, in its social and racial composition, and assumed the outward form of a mystery religion. So it appeared, not only to complete outsiders, like Pliny and Lucian, but to the inquirer and the potential catechumen.[1] It was a new religion, which had never been the public cultus of any tribe or nation. The Christian Church was a voluntary body, entered by a long and difficult process of initiation, but otherwise open to men, women, and children of any class, nationality, or race, including slaves and freedmen. Like other mystery religions, the Church had greater and lesser mysteries, the greater mysteries at Passover and Pentecost (and in some churches perhaps on the Sundays between these feasts), the lesser week by week through the rest of the year.

The greater mysteries were not repeated, but given once for all. That was remarkable, but not so singular as the rigour with which all baptized Christians abstained from all communion in sacrifices, and every other kind of active participation in the rituals of other religions. But the most fundamental difference between pagan and Christian mysteries must have been the most obscure to the

[1] See W. Weidlé, *The Baptism of Art*, 1949, especially pp. 22-5.

sympathetic outsider. The Christian expectation was not deliverance from this present world into a higher sphere beyond the stars. The Christian secret was not the way through the labyrinth to the life of the world to come, but the way to the risen life in Christ here and now. They were to present their bodies "as a living sacrifice, holy, acceptable to God," first "buried with Christ in baptism," then risen to newness of life in communion with Him. The Christian sacrifice was and is the whole life of the Church, prepared for martyrdom, which means witness, not only in death, but in the life of patience and love. No doubt the generality of early Christians expected swift and catastrophic changes in the order of this world. The next stage was the millennium, the reign of Christ and His saints on earth. This was not the end, but the beginning of the final, critical stage in history, in which the initiative in historical action would be theirs. That this might easily be misunderstood in the sense of a political revolution was probably one reason for the elaboration and secrecy of preparation for Christian baptism. The outcome indeed proved more complicated than the original expectation, and fresh adjustments were necessary; but the Christian churches accepted responsibility, when others were wringing their hands before social disintegration and decay, not because they "forsook eschatology," and changed their minds about the end of the world, but because they still believed, as they always had, that God was at work in history, leading all, in His own good time, to the final consummation.

To understand the Christians we must look first at their mysteries. The greater mysteries are baptism and the eucharist, or rather the baptismal eucharist, a single rite including what we should now call baptism, confirmation, and communion. Of this our earliest complete account is in the *Apostolic Tradition* of Hippolytus, which in the opinion of most modern scholars may be ascribed to a conservative party in the church of Rome in or about 220. But we have earlier brief descriptions in Justin Martyr and the *Didache*, and a large number of slighter references in the

literature of the second century. In fact
we know much more about the baptismal
eucharist than about the eucharist week by
week. This, as we shall see, is significant.
It will be useful to begin by reviewing the
description in the *Apostolic Tradition*.[1]

The candidates for baptism have been
instructed for a long time, three years in
most cases, and in the last three weeks
examined and exorcised day by day. They
have fasted on Friday and Saturday, and
received a further, very complicated exorcism from the hand of the Bishop of Rome.
They come to baptism bearing only their
own contribution to the eucharistic feast,
bread and perhaps something else, wine,
honey, or milk. They descend naked to
the water, where they renounce Satan, and
are anointed with oil of exorcism. In the
water they make their confession of faith
in the threefold name, and at each confession of belief in a person receive baptism.
As they come out of the stream they are
anointed again, this time with the oil of
thanksgiving. They dry themselves, put

[1] Ed. B. S. Easton, Cambridge, 1934, pp. 43–9; ed. G. Dix,
1937, pp. 29–43.

on their clothes, and receive a third anointing, with the seal of the cross, at the bishop's hand. Prayers follow and the kiss of peace. The bishop proceeds to "eucharist first the bread into the exemplum (which the Greeks call antitype) of the Flesh of Christ; and the cup mixed with wine for the antitype (which the Greeks call similitude) of the Blood which was shed for all who have believed in Him: and milk and honey mingled together in fulfilment of the promise to the Fathers, wherein He said, I will give you a land flowing with milk and honey; which Christ indeed gave, even His Flesh, whereby they who believe are nourished like little children, making the bitterness of the human heart sweet by the sweetness of His word; water also for an oblation for a sign of the laver, that the inner man also, which is psychic, may receive the same as the body."

Communion follows, not only in "the Bread of Heaven in Christ Jesus," but in water, milk (with honey in it), and finally wine from the chalice. "And they who partake shall taste of each cup thrice, he who gives it saying: 'In God the Father Almighty'; and he who receives shall say: 'Amen'. 'And in the Lord Jesus Christ'; and he shall say: 'Amen.' 'And in the Holy Spirit in the Holy Church'; and he shall say: 'Amen.' So shall it be done to each one.''

We need not suppose that this elaborate ritual was universal, or even common to the whole church of Rome. Some features may be peculiar to Hippolytus and his party, who were in schism from the rest of the Roman church at the time, though the ready adoption of his form, with only minor alterations, by several Eastern churches, hardly suggests that Hippolytus was eccentric in liturgical matters. What is really important is not the place of the bishop's sealing, or the relation of confirmation to baptism. The *Didache* and Justin do not mention oil at all, and the *Didascalia Apostolorum*, with other Syrian sources, puts the anointing and sealing before the bath.[1] The important thing, which is far more likely to be

---

[1] Ed. R. H. Connolly, Oxford, 1929, pp. xlix–l, 146–7; cf. the same editor's edition of *The Liturgical Homilies of Narsai*, Cambridge, 1909, pp. xl.–xlix.

common to all churches, is the unity of baptism and eucharist. This can be further illustrated from the paintings preserved in the Roman catacombs. Nearly all of them are of Biblical scenes, or scenes from pagan mythology, which in Christian circles had some sacramental reference, but all attempts to divide them between baptism and the eucharist break down. Some Protestant scholars have called them signs of salvation, but M. Wladimir Weidlé, a Russian Orthodox expert on the history of Christian art, has put his finger on the real point. "What has a Christian to do with any salvation but that which through a sacrament made him a Christian? . . . We can find the key to understand the early Church in general, and early Christian art in particular, only if we will refuse to divorce salvation and sacrament, even in thought."[1] The paintings represent not baptism alone, but conversion and baptism, completed by chrismation and communion, as it still is at the initiation of an Orthodox adult or infant.

[1] *Baptism of Art*, pp. 17–18.

When we look at the rite in this way as one continuous action, some of our theological problems vanish for a moment, to reappear as they must when we make a division. In the early Church the real presence was found not only in the eucharistic elements of bread and wine, but in milk and honey (called Christ's Flesh in the *Apostolic Tradition*), in the living water of baptism, and in the newly baptized who are buried and risen with Christ. No doubt if a Christian child asked where is Christ, the answer would be in the Body broken, "the Bread of Heaven in Christ Jesus," and in the Blood in the cup. The gift of the Holy Ghost was closely connected with the baptismal waters, the bishop's blessing, the seal, the holy oils. But Christ and the Holy Ghost were discerned as present in the entire rite. Catholic and Protestant answers to the problem of the real presence could both be given, without contradiction. It would be a mistake to interpret such words as exemplum, figura, antitypum, as they are applied to the eucharistic elements, in the sense of a metaphorical, not a real presence. It would be as much a mistake to assume a doctrine of the real presence or of transubstantiation.

It is the same with sacrifice. That the whole rite is a sacrificial mystery is beyond all question. The divine victim is Jesus Christ, in His Cross and passion, resurrection and ascension, in His Body broken and His Blood shed. But if we ask what is our offering, the baptized are sacrificed, buried with Him. Men and women, boys, girls, and babies are human sacrifices, dedicated in a literal sense to martyrdom. It was likely enough that many of the children would seal their baptism in blood. The baptized, and every communicant, bring their offerings with them, not only bread, but wine, milk, honey, cheese, olive oil, and olives. All are accepted, dedicated, to play their part in the sacrificial feast. All are offered in Christ, and made one with His sacrifice.

To imagine the baptismal eucharist in modern terms we must think not only of solemn baptisms, an inconvenient addition to the blessing of the font at the

Easter and Whitsun vigils in the Western rites. It may be more helpful to think of other sacraments and sacramentals set in a eucharistic context after the baptismal model since primitive times. Ordinations in the Anglican Church are commonly confined to cathedrals, which is unfortunate, since they too are human sacrifices in a eucharistic setting. In the Middle Ages the nuptial mass had a like character. The bride and bridegroom knelt together in the presbytery, between the altar and the choir, under a pall for their dedication. This pall was directly descended from the veil which in pagan Rome covered the bride but not the bridegroom. In pre-Christian ritual she alone was the victim. In Christian marriage both are sacrificed, in one another in Christ. A more familiar modern example is the coronation. The Queen is a sacrificed sacred person. Anointed, crowned, and lifted as a victim to the throne, she makes her offering, first in the elements of bread and wine, then in "a pall or altar-cloth . . . and an ingot or wedge of gold of a pound weight," which the Archbishop receives and places with the elements upon the altar. The prayers of the Church follow, as they did in the early Church immediately after baptism. The consecration and communion continue as part of the same action.

The effect of the coronation on those of our fellow citizens who are not Christians seems to me interesting and important. There are many signs that the entire action spoke to something very deeply rooted in them. For the first time the eucharist had a meaning, not only for the Church but for the nation. The idea of sacrifice came alive as the Queen offered herself and her peoples in the sacrifice of Christ.

I think this might happen more often. But before we consider how this might be done we need to examine the difference between the eucharist as we know it and the baptismal eucharist of the primitive Church. In the early Church the weekly eucharist was a repetition in part of the baptismal rite. The weekly offering was concentrated in bread and wine as the Paschal offering was not, but the idea of

an offering of the whole Church, of every
communicant as dedicated in baptism to
death and resurrection, could never be
absent from the centre of consciousness
in the days of persecution. The nexus of
baptism and the eucharist remains alive
in the Eastern churches, not only through
the communion of infants immediately
after baptism, but much more through
the common practice of infant
communion in the weekly liturgy. More
often than not infants are the only communicants, and this gives to every adult,
when he does make his communion, a
sense that he is renewing his baptismal
dedication, and recovering infant inno-
cency. Whatever objections may be made
to these practices—and the objections are
serious—there can be little doubt that
their place in the Eastern tradition has
played an important part in avoiding, or
at least postponing, controversies about
sacrifice which have troubled us in the
West.

For if the eucharist is regarded as a
distinct rite existing by itself, the problem
of what we ourselves offer becomes acute.

In most of the Eastern and some of the Gallican rites the elements are regarded as an icon of Christ, and treated with considerable ceremony before consecration, in the rite of the prothesis, at the very beginning of the service, and at the Great Entrance, before consecration and communion. A like language is used in the Roman offertory prayers, but here it is less obtrusive, and more continuous with the oblation of the elements in the first half of the canon of the mass, for Roman conservatism kept the preparation of the elements in the old position, almost immediately before the consecration. The idea of a moment when the elements become Christ's Body and Blood grew up slowly, but quite inevitably. I see no evidence of controversy between East and West about consecration by the epiclesis of the Holy Ghost, or by the words of Christ in the institution of the sacrament, until the middle of the thirteenth century.[1] Just before that time the rubrics

[1] Manuel, Great Rhetor of the Church of Constantinople, in his reply to Friar Francis (c. 1240), *Patrologia Graeca*, 140 c. 481, seems a clear case. I am not at all certain that

were being introduced, in province after province of the West, which provide for the elevations of the Host and the Chalice, and the adoration of the Body and Blood of Christ, at Christ's words of institution, in the middle of the canon.

The history of this innovation, which spread slowly in the last quarter of the twelfth and the first quarter of the thirteenth century, is in some ways still very obscure.[1] It seems to me simpler to assume that a general demand for a moment of consecration was resolved by splitting the difference between six invocations, than to suppose any hostility to the idea of a consecration by invocation or epiclesis. The Gallican and Mozarabic masses contain alternative invocations of the Holy Ghost, of Christ, and of the

---

Theodore of Andida, who may be earlier, had a controversial intention, *ibid.*, c. 452–3. The controversy did not develop until the middle of the fourteenth century, when it became a major issue in the writings of Nicholas Cabasilas.

[1] Documentation in H. R. Gummey, *The Consecration of the Eucharist*, Philadelphia, 1908, pp. 395–9. See E. Dumoutet, *Le Désir de voir l'Hostie*, Paris, 1926, and, for a Protestant view, T. W. Drury, *Elevation in the Eucharist*, Cambridge, 1907.

Holy Trinity on different feasts[1] at a similar place to the Eastern epicleses of the Holy Ghost, and the prayer of the angel (*supplices te rogamus*) in the Roman canon, which at one time fulfilled the same function.[2]

What is important is not the place of the consecration, but the effect upon Western piety of the idea of a double offering, of bread and wine before, and of the Body and Blood after the decisive words are spoken. It may be that this idea is older than the rubrics for the elevation, and played some part in giving rise to them. There can be no doubt that the change in ritual made the idea far more general, and that the theology of the mass in the later Middle Ages turned on the idea of an actual sacrifice of the Body and Blood of Christ, not of an icon or figure of Christ to be transformed

[1] See H. R. Gummey, *op. cit.*, pp. 334–57. Examples can easily be found in the Mozarabic *Missale Mixtum* in *Patrologia Latina* 85, e.g. c. 304, 329, 353.

[2] See Edmund Bishop's appendices to *The Liturgical Homilies of Narsai*, especially pp. 152–3, and a note by S. Salaville to his translation of Nicholas Cabasilas, *Explication de la Divine Liturgie*, Paris, 1943, pp. 171–8.

in the offering into the Body and Blood.[1]

This is the idea which the Reformers repudiated. In so doing they were in danger of repudiating the whole idea of sacrifice in the eucharist. But we may doubt if they went so far as they themselves supposed. What is irreverently called the "funeral tea" notion of Holy Communion at least assumes a very real connection between the sacrifice of the death of Christ and the eucharistic feast. The idea that the eucharist is "not a sacrifice, but a feast upon a sacrifice,"[2] is compatible with belief in the real presence, not only in faithful receivers, but in the elements. Everything depends on what we mean by "a true and proper sacrifice." Such language has been used by those who emphatically repudiated any belief in a real presence in the elements themselves

[1] I should regard the condemnation of Berengar of Tours in the eleventh century as the defeat of an attempt to make this latter view explicit. But the word "transubstantiation" does not appear before the twelfth century, and its logical meaning was not developed until the thirteenth.

[2] So Ralph Cudworth (1617–87) and Simon Patrick (1626–1707), from whom the idea probably passed into the proposals for a revised Prayer Book in 1688–9.

before communion. It was so used in the
seventeenth and eighteenth centuries by
Anglicans like Heylin and Hickes, Dod-
well and John Johnson, who were
eirenical about the eucharistic sacrifice,
but not at all eirenical about transubstantiation, or anything resembling such
a doctrine. On the other hand it is possible for a Lutheran to affirm the real
presence in the sense of consubstantiation,
and yet to repudiate all idea of a eucharistic sacrifice as distinct from our feeding
on the sacrifice of the cross. But this
itself makes the meal sacrificial.

It would be a mistake to ascribe all
eucharistic controversies to a confusion of
language. Yet it seems an inescapable fact
that we have all misunderstood one
another more or less radically in the last
four centuries, not least within the Anglican communion. Were we wrong to
repudiate medieval eucharistic doctrine?
The present tendency in the church of
Rome is to do the same, for something
like the same reason. Roman Catholic
theology of late years has laid more and
more stress not only on the identity of the

mass with the sacrifice of Christ, but on the continuity of action between the offertory and the consecration, on the basic identity of consecration and offering. The idea of a moment of consecration is not repudiated, for such an idea, once entertained, can hardly be avoided, nor can the moment be displaced without offence to devotion. If we say that there is no consecration apart from communion, we are involved in some similar difficulties, which would cease to be of practical importance only if non-communicating attendance were altogether barred. What is important is to avoid the notion of a double offering, first of bread and wine, and then of the Body and Blood of Christ; and this is easier for Anglicans than in the Roman communion, because the Church of England has not inherited a canon which is older than the idea of a moment of consecration. Why then do Anglicans throw away their advantages by inserting a prayer of oblation between consecration and communion?

The answer is that their own prayer of consecration seems in some way inadequate and jejune. It needs to be supplemented. Some provinces of the Anglican communion have enlarged it, on what we may broadly call orientalizing lines, by doubling or postponing the consecration, and including a memorial of the whole work of Christ, which will also serve as a prayer of offering, between the words of institution and the epiclesis of the Holy Ghost. But in England this does not commend itself to popular piety, partly at least because the connection between the words of institution and the moment of consecration is deeply rooted in eight centuries of tradition and devotion. The Church of England might be wise to accept this tradition as a datum, and return to the older Anglican custom, still observed in Evangelical and in many moderate churches, of proceeding with the minimum of interruption from consecration to communion.

This need not imply satisfaction with the present prayer of consecration, which could and should be amplified, especially in the commemoration of the resurrection and ascension of Christ. But in any future

revision there will be irresistible pressure
to allow the use of the old prayer in conservative congregations. This would not
much matter, if the revised prayer had the
same structure, but if at the very centre of
the eucharistic rite there were alternative
prayers of consecration as different from
one another as the present prayer and the
South African canon, the division between
Anglican congregations would become a
good deal more definite, and perhaps
more acute.

The use of the prayer of oblation after
the prayer of consecration, instead of in
its Prayer Book place after the communion, need not imply any further
sacrifice of the Body and Blood of Christ,
but behind some of the arguments used
in its favour it is difficult not to detect a
notion that the defect in the Prayer Book
rite is the absence of any oblation of consecrated gifts. If this is a defect, then we
must think the Reformers radically wrong
in their criticism of the medieval doctrine
of the Mass. Moreover it seems to me that
we must criticize some in the modern
liturgical movement as in danger of

obscuring the most distinctive feature of the Roman rite, which, so far as I can discover, is the only traditional liturgy to possess an explicit oblation of the elements after the consecration has been completed.

I do not doubt that the Anglican Reformers made many mistakes. Their principal error in the Order of Communion was the omission of any reference to the oblation of bread and wine. This was in part repaired at the last revision in 1662, where rubrics for the preparation of the elements were inserted in two places, before the prayer of the Church, and before the consecration, but neither place quite fits the liturgical action, and neither rubric has ever been universally observed. Where the influence of the liturgical movement is felt there has been some agitation for the revival of the offertory procession, in which all the communicants would make their offerings, in bread or in bread and wine. But if this is done before the prayer for the Church the result is to emphasize the difference between this oblation from people and priest and the eucharistic consecration. No one wants to make the offertory after the sanctus, which is now recognized as a primitive and important part of the prayer of consecration itself. It would seem to be more in line with Anglican tradition to relate the offertory procession, if there is one, to the approach of the communicants to the altar before the general confession, and to treat the prayer for the Church as part of the preliminary rite, corresponding to the prayers of the faithful at the end of the ancient synaxis, the synagogue service. This in fact corrresponds to the common custom whereby those who do not intend to stay for the communion withdraw not before, but after, the prayer for the Church Militant.

These are modest and conservative suggestions. But I do not believe that the Paschal mystery will be revealed again in all its glory unless we are prepared for a more radical change. I should like to see the liturgy of the faithful at least sometimes divided from the synagogue service. At Mattins and Evensong we have enough of lessons, psalmody, and sermon. We could sometimes dispense with the epistle and gospel at a nuptial mass, or when baptism or confirmation are celebrated with the eucharist. Ordination in the Anglican rite is a very impressive service, but it repels congregations by its excessive prolixity. This could be reduced if we allowed the Litany, perhaps abbreviated, to be our prayer for the Church, and continued with the offertory, consecration, and communion immediately after the ordination. In this case the epistle and gospel have become associated in action with the ordination of deacons and priests, but baptism has its own gospel and prayers, and could lead even more directly into the eucharist. I should like to see a bishop use his *jus liturgicum* to continue after a confirmation with the Nicene creed and then the rest of the Communion. So week by week the eucharist could be related to the other sacraments, to the offering of souls and bodies in complete and utter dedication to the service of Christ.

I do not mean to suggest that without this the eucharist is not a sacrifice. The sacramental feast has been celebrated by itself from the first days of the Church, but never without relation to the passion and resurrection of Christ, and to the sacrament of baptism. Our need to make this relation more explicit has become more acute in an age when sacrifice has lost its primary part in human life. Sacrifice cannot mean much unless it means everything, an utter selfgiving in complete union with the Lord's passion.

# Chapter V: Sacrifice and Atonement

TO many of our contemporaries sacrifice is not only a difficult but a repulsive idea. The slaughter of hundreds and thousands of innocent animals to appease the gods is a horrible notion. More abhorrent, because more inconsistent, is the strange idea that an all-merciful and all-loving God would accept the slaughter of His innocent Son as a substitute for all shortcomings in obedience to Him. Such ideas, they say, must have a pathological origin. If they are themselves sympathetic, not only to Christian ethics, but to Jesus Christ as teacher, leader, and master, they will allow that He accepted sacrifice, with many other historical institutions of His world, and that He saw His own death in sacrificial terms. He founded an unbloody and innocent rite to sublimate the impulses that had led men to sacrifice, and to turn them into the enacted recollection of His life and death. This in its time did great good, yet the use of sacrificial language in reference to the eucharist opened the way inevitably to a slipping back into carnal and magical ways of regarding divine power, into thoughts of Christ's Body and Blood as made present on our altars to be immolated again, and offered by us for our own selfish ends. Zwingli was therefore right to say that we cannot, without peril, take "This is My Body" and "This is My Blood" in a literal sense. But the Reformers should have gone further, and rejected not only sacrifice in the eucharist but sacrifice in the death of Christ. They were held back by too devout an attachment to the literal meaning of Biblical texts, and the Reformation could not be completed until the atonement was understood simply as the great example of a loving life and an innocent death.

I have put these objections deliberately in a very moderate form, as they are advanced by many who do acknowledge Jesus as master and Lord, though they would not call him God in the sense of the creeds. But we all know that there are many who would go much further, and reject the Christian religion because it is inextricably entangled in the sacrificial idea. Mrs. Margaret Knight for instance said in one of her recent broadcasts:

> Any modern child must feel that there is something morally wrong in the idea of God giving his only Son as a sacrifice, as the price of man's redemption. That idea wasn't strange 2,000 years ago, when sacrifices in temples were taken as a matter of course. It's not only strange today, it's abhorrent. What would you say to a child who had the courage to reject the whole idea? [1]

This is not a new objection. It is many years now since J. S. Mill, for substantially the same reason, said:

> I will call no being good, who is not what I mean when I apply that epithet to my fellow-creatures; and if such a being can sentence me to hell for not calling him so, to hell I will go. [2]

The cross is a scandal, "a stone of stumbling and a rock of offence" which we all try to get round. But how much of

---

[1] *Listener*, January 27th, 1955.
[2] In his *Examination of Sir William Hamilton's Philosophy*, 1867 ed., p. 124.

the objection to the Christian sacrifice is
directed against sacrifice itself, and how
much against a misleading presentation of
the sacrificial idea? We certainly could not
hope that the scandal would be removed if
the cross were better understood. It might
even be intensified. But it is our business to
do all that we can to ensure that the rock of
offence is Christ himself, and not a figment
of the theological imagination.

It is here, I believe, that the modern
science of comparative religion must be
our ally and not our fear. Most objections
to the idea of sacrifice, like Mrs. Knight's,
turn first upon ransom. They are rooted in
the belief that the primary meaning is tri-
bute or propitiation paid for human weakness and sin to the justice of gods. As we
shall see, the idea of propitiation cannot
simply be cut out, but it does seem to me
of immense importance that sacrifice is
not in the first place an offering out of
our income to a divine landlord, or even a
fine paid for arrears of rent. There is a
great and growing volume of evidence to
show that the idea of sacrifice is older
than the idea of private property, that

beasts were slain ritually not in the first place to feed the gods or to avert their wrath by making a scapegoat of an innocent substitute, but because the beasts themselves were regarded as holy manifestations of divine energy and life. They could be slain, but only with reverence and by permission. In many lonely villages, where there was no shrine or organized priesthood, the corn itself was treated in the same way. The first corn, and the first or last sheaf of the harvest, were themselves regarded as images of the corn maiden, and venerated in the fields at harvest time. The corn was offered to the corn, herself to herself.[1]

The modern analogue to this is not, as some have thought, the filling in of a form to record the yield of the harvest, and the grin of satisfaction on the farmer's face as he seals it up to post to a committee. We shall get much nearer to the primitive feeling if we think of a child picking a bunch of flowers, taking it

[1] See Jane Harrison, *Ancient Art and Ritual*, pp. 67–71, J. G. Frazer, *Spirits of the Corn and of the Wild*, 1912, vol. i, pp. 150–70, vol. ii, pp. 47–65.

home and putting it in water, feeling some sense of guilt when the flowers fade and die, and if he (or she) is an imaginative and tender-hearted child, either burying them in the garden or pressing one of them and laying it up in a book, a private shrine. Our first impulse is to treasure effectual signs of grace and favour, and to adore the divinity in them. But to keep them for our own we have to store them, and therefore, very often, we kill and bury them, in some dim hope that they will rise again.

I think S. Paul had something like this in mind when he wrote in the Epistle to the Romans of a childhood of man between Adam and Moses, when sin was not as yet made plain. Men met God and made offerings to Him without any regular cultus, any religious law. The law was added "because of transgressions," "that sin might be made exceeding sinful." Law, and the sense of obligation in religion, develops and intensifies our own sense of guilt. For this reason sacrifice becomes a sin-offering. The idea of propitiation took a specially strong hold on the people of Israel, because they had been given a particular, a specialized sense of awe at the holiness of God, and the gulf between God's goodness and the pride and sin of contumacious men. It would be too much to say that the idea of communion with God, of the renewal of the covenant between the Lord and His people, completely disappeared from the Jewish sacrifices; but it was overlaid, as in no other nation so far as I know, by the idea of an offering in propitiation for the sins of the whole people, as well as of particular persons. There was no element of augury in Jewish sacrifices, no divination of God's will in the flesh of the victim. The victim itself was sacred, but not divine, from the time, whenever that was, when an imageless worship entirely excluded the worship of God in the form of a bull.

That extraordinary person, Simone Weil, herself a Jewess who hesitated on the edge of the Roman Catholic Church, was convinced that the Jews were religiously inferior to their neighbours, especially the Egyptians. They were predestined to reject Christ, and this predestination was shown in their continual hostility to the idea of a suffering god.[1] If we adopt this notion to the exclusion of our traditional belief that Israel was the chosen vessel in whom alone Messias could be born, I am sure that we shall go very seriously wrong. But I think Simone Weil did take hold of a very important complementary idea, which is not quite so untraditional as she herself supposed. It has links with the line of thought to be found in the *Epistle of Barnabas* and other early patristic writings, where Christians urge that the Jews have persistently misunderstood, throughout their history, the real meaning of law and prophecy. In our reading of the Old Testament we need to see not only preparation for Christ, but the gathering storm that would lead to His crucifixion. In our effort, as historians, to see the religion of Israel with the eyes of the Israelites, we must not fall back, as Christians have often fallen, into seeing

[1] See her *Lettre à un religieux*, 1951, Eng. trans., *Letter to a Priest*, 1953.

our own religion from their point of view.

In course of time the Levitical sacrifices were more and more assimilated in thought to the whole mass of religious and secular observances which constituted the Jewish law. The devout Jew kept the Torah, in Palestine or in the dispersion. He could sacrifice only in Jerusalem, and he could not always get there even for the Passover. All his observances therefore became, and still are, sacrificial in his own peculiar sense, offerings of his whole intention in conformity with the will of God. This is both the glory and the burden of Judaism. As S. Paul felt and said, it fostered self-righteousness, and could never take away sin. It also made the idea of a revelation of God in a suffering man an impossible stumbling-block, a rock of offence.

In the Hellenistic world the line of development was in the opposite direction. As men became more and more aware of the plurality of divine manifestations in any and every part of the world, they were less and less inclined to regard their gods and goddesses as lords and ladies of the lands, givers of rain and sun and shower. Meteorology was, for the wise at least, a philosopher's business, not unmixed with astrological science. The gods of the cities and the Roman empire still received their sacrifices, but there was much more genuine religious feeling in rites intended to establish communion with powers at large who might assist the worshipper in this life and the world to come, demons of the earth and air, good physicians like Aesculapius, spirits who attend on childbirth or who know the way to a better land in the realms of the dead. To many philosophers this was indeed foolishness, and Christianity another and grosser form of the same foolishness. No doubt Christians had the key to some kind of oriental magic. Otherwise the obstinacy of their martyrs could not be explained. But the worship of a crucified man was the last and most absurd form of ridiculous hero-worship.

Therefore the whole effort of Christian thought, from the time when the divorce between Christianity and Judaism was finally accomplished, was devoted to establishing, to their own satisfaction and that of others, the critical truth that Christ was no demi-god, but the Creator of the world manifest in the flesh. Communion with God through Christ was not communion with a genie, but union with God, the God of Israel and the ultimate Being of philosophic speculation, not a god like the gods of the mysteries and the local deities of particular shrines. The interest of the controversies against Gnosticism and Marcionism, and of the later Arian and Christological controversies, does not seem to me to have been primarily metaphysical. The problem was not to make a satisfactory map of the cosmos, but to protect the gospel of salvation from misunderstandings which would make it no more than a means of obtaining a special kind of *mana*, of ascending to a superior level of spiritual being, either through union with a demigod changed into a special kind of flesh, and changing our flesh into flesh of this superior sort, or through the communication of a special spiritual inspiration from

113

man to man. Those who fought for the Nicene definition that the Son of God is of one substance with the Father were equally concerned to protect the integrity of Christ's manhood, for if the Son of God is a semi-divine being, neither God nor man, "What He did not assume, He did not redeem." If the Word of God dwelt in Mary's son, but in such a way that the birth, death, and resurrection of Christ belong to the man, not to the Word, once again there is no saving victim, no action and suffering of God in the flesh. Indeed the salutation of the Son as equal to the Father, and of Mary as Mother of God, are in an important sense secondary issues, as can be seen by the survival of an element of what is called subordinationism in some orthodox theologies of the Trinity, as well as in differences between orthodox Christians about the place of Mary in the economy of salvation.

All the theological controversies of the early Church proceeded on the background of a presupposition common to Christian and pagan religion, but obscure in Judaism, that gods, if gods there are,

commune with men through the flesh of
a saving victim. There was no need to
prove that Christ's death was a sacrifice,
if He Who suffered on the cross was God
in man. That became a problem in a very
much later period, when other sacrifices
than the Christian had almost completely
disappeared from the Christian world,
but not so far away, beyond the Pyrenees,
a great culture and an impressive religion
were reaching their second zenith without
any sacrifices at all. Islam, not Judaism,
is the great example of an unsacrificial
religion, rooted in the rejection of all
agricultural ritual. It would be very interesting to survey the effects of this on
agriculture in the Middle East,[1] but we
must not be deflected from our main
purpose by an examination of the merits
and defects of Islam. What is important
for us is that part that Islam played in
forcing Christian theologians to develop
for the first time a theory of sacrifice, a
doctrine of the atonement, to explain
why God should choose such an odd and
painful way of meeting with man.

[1] See W. Ramsay, *Luke the Physician*, 1908, pp. 105–98.

What we may call the traditional
Western theory of the atonement was
conceived in a feudal civilization in feudal
terms. God is the Supreme Lord, to
Whom infinite services are due. We
are all hopelessly behindhand with our
obligations to the Supreme Suzerain, Who
is just as well as loving, and must insist
on some discharge of all duties. His
beloved Son has consented of His own
free will to become our proper representative, to bear all our burdens, and to set
us right with the heavenly court. So far all
this has to do with the illustration of
divine history in contemporary metaphor,
something which had been done before in
a less systematic way, in sermons and
hymns,[1] and must always be done in
popular expositions.

S. Anselm in his *Cur Deus Homo* was
more rational and more ambitious. He
sought not only to sing the triumph of
Christ, but also to "justify the ways of
God to men." But it seems to me that his
presentation suffers not only from its

[1] See the patristic material collected by Bishop Gustav
Aulen in *Christus Victor*, Eng. trans., 1931.

inevitable involvement in contemporary language, but also from the limitation of his information on the subject of sacrifice to the Old Testament, the Epistles of S. Paul and the Epistle to the Hebrews (which he regarded as S. Paul's). He was too much caught up in the Jewish background, where the sacrificed victim is an offering to God, but not a means whereby God reveals His secret intentions. There are no auspices. Abelard, who was better read in the classics, at least saw what he had missed. Abelard's modern defenders have generally forgotten that he was a poet as well as a professor. It is a mistake to think that in his mind an *exemplum* means purely and simply a moral example. To all poets an image, example, or type is more than a metaphor. It is charged with a mystery that cannot be revealed in any other way. So Abelard saw in the crucifixion a mysterious type, an *exemplum*, of the divine self-sacrificing love, kindling and enflaming ours.[1]

S. Anselm had more influence, and

---

[1] So in his *Exposition of the Epistle to the Romans* Patrologia Latina 178, c. 836.

much of it was bad, not by his own fault, but because social changes in the next two hundred years transformed the sense of the Latin *debitum* from a due to a debt, from a service, symbolical, military, or servile, into a financial obligation, frequently commuted for a lump sum. God, to S. Anselm, was "a great king above all the earth," a fountain of justice who requires our whole allegiance. But in another generation this great receiver of services had become a universal creditor. God was inevitably figured in the likeness of His vicar, whose financial demands were more accurately and professionally calculated than those of other lords, and whose privileges and exemptions, though very bountiful, were mysteriously bestowed, much more generously on religious communities than on parish churches and their poor curates.

The emphasis on offering in medieval religion found its root and centre in the mass. Indeed the experience of offering Mass was possibly more important for S. Anselm's idea of the atonement than his feudal allegiances or his meditations on the book of Leviticus and the Epistle to the Romans. All these went together and sustained each other, for the mass in the monasteries was, among other things, their form of service to their benefactors, and to the whole kingdom in which they served. They held their tenures by prayer, and "more especially by the acceptable sacrifice of the altar." They thought of themselves as Levites, a priestly class, fulfilling Old Testament types, with the Pope as their High Priest on earth and Christ as High Priest in heaven. Communion indeed remained the climax for the priest as his mass, but for the worshippers the central moment was consecration and offering, the immolation at priestly hands of an acceptable victim. As dues and services were more exactly calculated, so were these offerings, with a view to the weight of merits on celestial weighing-machines, which had a key place in the medieval scheme of church decoration.

This was but a phase in the history of the Christian religion. I would not be so unjust as to suppose that the Western

Catholic conception of the sacrifice of the mass is, or ever was, bounded and limited by feudalism. But some developments in doctrine and more in practice were conditioned by it, and are still hard to escape. The real bar to the progress of the liturgical movement in the Roman Catholic Church is not, as we have lately discovered, the discipline of fasting and confession before communion, for these can be modified. It is not the eastward position, or even the Latin liturgy, for these may be altered. It is much more likely to be the customs and revenues associated with requiems.

These have had lasting consequences not only for Roman Catholicism, where correctives have been found through the slow return of general communion in the eucharist, but for the Reformed Churches, where the sacrifice of the mass was rejected only to make the cross into something very like a medieval requiem mass, a propitiatory offering for the living and the dead, without reference to the resurrection and ascension, and with only an occasional connection between sacrifice and communion. The nature of Christ's propitiation became the subject of a scholastic exegesis in direct descent from medieval exegesis of the mass. The effects of His atonement were conceived as operating in His elect by a chain of necessary causes as mechanical and complicated as the effects of the mass on departed souls in medieval speculations. The privileges of the elect were defined on the pattern of monastic exemptions from all jurisdiction but the Pope's. They are in the place of the privileged orders, who indeed had sometimes claimed a like assurance of eternal salvation.

When absolute predestination fell out of fashion the conditions of acceptance, conversion, and regeneration became the subject of as rigorous a discipline, still based on a fundamentally feudal notion that God gives or refuses grace by a kind of land conveyance, either simply by His inscrutable will, as in developed Calvinism, or to tenants prepared to accept His conditions, as in Arminianism. The seed-bed of all this thinking is the feudal estate, which was still in being in most parts of

Europe in the eighteenth century. But we have also to admit that it is quite honestly "Biblical," based on interpretations of texts in S. Paul that are coloured not only by contemporary social conditions, but by those very texts in Leviticus to which he appeals. This is the really frightening thing, because it underlines our danger of making the same kind of mistake.

We think and speak in a civilization that is decidedly and, I think, finally post-feudal, that thinks of history not in terms of the rise and fall of dynasties, but of the development and decay of cultures, and behind that the evolutionary process. No philosophy of history will satisfy us that does not take into account the paintings in the caves and the record of the rocks. We have a far more difficult task in interpreting the New Testament than S. Anselm, whose society was in most material respects very near to Jerusalem and Nazareth, to shepherds and flocks, ears of corn, fish and fishers of men, high priests and temple dues. On the other hand we have more material, not only in our more detailed archaeological knowledge of the immediate background of the New Testament, but through our more extensive acquaintance with comparative religion.

It seems to me that we must go back to an emphasis first of all on Christ as the saving victim, the very image of God, revealing in His life and death the kind of love that God is and has for the creatures whom He made to live their lives in all the intricate and infinite variety of their individual and corporate being, that they might so learn to love and serve Him. That kind of love which is not compulsion but creation into freedom must involve sympathy and suffering, in the sense of willing exposure to be acted upon. The impassible became passible, not out of necessity, because of sin, but out of love, because of creation. Is the cross then no sin-offering, no propitiation? I think we must read S. Paul's words[1] in their immediate context, as in the margin of the Revised Version:

> Whom God set forth to be propitiatory, through faith in his blood, to show his righteousness (because

[1] Romans 3, vv. 25–6.

of the passing over of the sins done aforetime,
in the forbearance of God); for the showing of his
righteousness in the present season, that he might
himself be just and the justifier of him that hath
faith in Jesus.

This is S. Paul interpreting a chapter of
Leviticus in the light of the sacrifice of
Christ, and thereby affording some temptation to others to interpret the cross by
Leviticus and the day of atonement. But
everywhere in these chapters, and above
all here, his main theme is present, that
the law was given to make sin and righteousness plain. So sacrifice became an
institution, and Christ was crucified at
Passover time, to reveal to men not only
God's love, but their sin.

Behind the image of the day of atonement in S. Paul and in the Epistle to the
Hebrews is the image of another sin-
offering that was in the mind of the
early Church at an even earlier date,
and according to all four Evangelists,
was on Our Lord's own lips in speaking
of Himself before His passion. The song
of the suffering servant tells of a sacrificed victim whose slayers did not know

124

that they were sacrificing for their own
sins and the sins of many others.

> He grew up as a sapling,
> And as a root from an arid soil;

like the spirit of vegetation. But he was
not an object of ritual reverence. Rather

> As one from whom men avert their gaze,
> He was despised, and we regarded him not.

He was borne along to the slaughter, not
as a sacrificed victim, but

> As a ewe before her shearers,
> He was dumb, and opened not his mouth.

And yet

> Truly he gave himself as a guilt-offering.
> My servant shall bring justification to many,
> And their iniquities he will bear.

In the end he will appear as a royal
victim, restored after his humiliation:

> Therefore will I assign him the many for his
>     portion,
> And numberless shall be his spoil;
> Because he laid bare his soul unto death,
> And with the rebellious he was numbered;
> But he bare the sin of many,
> And for the rebellious he interposed.[1]

[1] Isaiah 53, vv. 2–12. I have taken my translation from
C. R. North, *The Suffering Servant in Deutero-Isaiah*,
Oxford, 1948, pp. 121–2.

This imagery is not derived from Levitical ritual, and yet it is sacrificial. It is coloured by other sacrifices, by the cutting of corn, the shearing and slaughter of of sheep, and the humiliation of the divine king. It is significant that among the historical figures who have been identified with the servant in ancient and modern times are Uzziah, Hezekiah, Josiah, Jehoiachin, and Zerubbabel.[1] But Tammuz and Osiris are as appropriate. The poem is a criticism of all rituals, pointing to a sufficient offering who will not be recognized as a sacrificed victim by those who put him to death.

He offers himself for those who kill him, and in this sense is priest and victim at his own sacrifice. But his slayers also have their part in the action. His death is for them, and for "many" like them. (In Levitical sacrifices those for whom the sacrifice was offered normally slew the victim.) If we follow Christ, as He is represented to us in the Gospels, in using

[1] See the references under these names in C. R. North, *op. cit.*, a valuable historical survey of Jewish and Christian exegesis.

this figure to interpret His sacrifice, it seems to me that we shall find here the clue to the problem of our participation. No other religion than the Christian has taken half so seriously the solidarity of all men in guilt, of the slayers of Christ with those who stoned the prophets, and of Christians with the crowds who shouted "Hosanna" and "crucify," with the Apostles who followed and fled. When we make our communion, Christ puts Himself into our hands, and we handle Him. We are the same human beings, the same sinners who killed Him. We cannot touch the image of God without doing Him violence. But He lets us do it. He has said "Father, forgive them," and He gives us communion.

The scandal of the cross is to be forgiven, not only for our own sins, but for the sin of man. In this sense Christ is a sin-offering, by sinners for sinners, "made to be sin on our behalf." But He is not a substitute, drawing down upon Himself the whole burden of divine wrath. His forgiveness is free, because we can never deserve it, but it is not a release from the burden of flesh, from desire, or from judgment. We who are baptized into Christ—and in this sense not only once, but continually in the eucharist—are baptized into His death, nailed to His cross, that we may look from thence for the resurrection of the flesh and the life of the world to come.